Scrap Paper Poetry

Dean Wood

BookLeaf Publishing

India | USA | UK

Presentation by *BookLeaf Publishing*

Web: www.bookleafpub.com

E-mail: info@bookleafpub.com

ISBN: 9789358362411

First edition 2021

For you – thank you for holding a piece of my mind and cradling it in your hands

PREFACE

This is a collection of poems that I hope make you question the world around you. They touch on subjects such as feminism, loss, love, science, fate, and personal identity. There is even some character Easter Eggs for you to find. I wrote many of these poems in the margins of school notes, on the back of worksheets, on post-it notes, and in numerous notebooks. Some were written on my phone when paper just wasn't available.

I wonder how much of yourself you will find in these pages and these words. Enjoy the journey and the exploration.

Excelsior.

- Dean Wood

1.

for centuries

humanity looked at the horizon and

wondered

> *what's out there*

looked at the ocean and wondered

> *what's down there*

looking at the stars and wondered

> *what's out there*

but we never looked inside and

wondered

> *who's in here*

- exploration

2.

don't call me pretty
don't call me smart
i've been cute since i was three
and clever since i was six

tell me how i am independent
tell me stories of my heart
i've been fightin' to be me
and i had to learn how to listen

show me how i make you laugh
show me how i brighten the day
my humour isn't exactly normal
and my smile doesn't make birds sing

just please
for the love of God

tell me i'm worth more than my face

tell me i'm worth something more

     - what i see in the mirror can't be the

only thing that matters

3.

feather touches graze the side of his
neck
he flinches at the soft sensation
his skin is equal parts bruises and scars
his heart and soul are worse; beaten
and scared
furious anger beats at the edges of
every movement
and terrible loneliness hangs in his eyes
he is more thunderstorm than boy
his skin stretches to try and contain
the storm
sometimes it breaks and the results
beautiful tragedies
every single one
he is gunpowder and hurricane and sin
everything mothers warn to avoid

his hands are rough and know just how

to create the world

and tear it down to size

equally comfortable holding a gun or

a blade

he is a dangerous juxtaposition

of good looks and gasoline

don't break him

- good looks and gasoline

4.

if i thought i could get away with it

i'd kill time and poison fear and
stab loneliness

forget the meaning of my responsibilities
and shake the tree

if only i could kill time

                              - time kills us all

5.

our universe is 13.8 billion years old

our galaxy 13.5 billion

our planet is 4.5 billion years old

humans have been on the Earth for

200,000 years

    time is meaningless when

    emotions are at play

humans say we will love each other

forever

    but nothing last forever less one

    day

    but time is irrelevant

    and the universe proves over and

    over

    that anything is possible

    no matter how improbable

so maybe love can last forever plus

one day

- nothing can last forever except maybe

love

6.

Children children ever playing.
Father father ever spraying
the crops for the later haying.
Mother mother is always saying,

'Come away, come away, come away
from the water.
Just wait until the weather is hotter.
Run farther, run farther, run farther than
the daughter.
Cover your ears and close your eyes
from the slaughter.'

Parents parents ever working.
Boys boys ever lurking
in the shadows they are smirking.
Mother mother is always overlooking.

Go away, go away, go away to the

battle.

Father cannot leave his cattle.

Race towards, race towards the rattle

as Sister dashes to tattle.

Brother's lies will be found

but not before the sound

of twenty-one guns is crowned

and his body lies in the ground.

- enlisted

7.

the wonders grow tall and children
laugh.
you feel your face crack into a smile and
hysterical laughter fills the air.
the world gets more and more
fantastical as you walk
farther and farther from where you
started.

butterflies tickle your skin and fireflies
light the way.
lanterns line the path. take the time to
smell the roses along the way.
breathe in the toxic scent and forget
your worries, your problems.
wonderland is here.

follow the rabbit, white as snow;

nothing will stop you 'til you reach the
goal.
go on, follow. your heart begs you so.

what's your name? where are you from?
Where have you been?
the caterpillar won't help you.
those beautiful roses tear at your skin
and clothes.
"never will you make it out." a slimy
voice takes root "you are mine."
the sky darkens and thunder cracks.
screams replace laughs.

tears make rivers down your cheeks as
you succumb
to sleep.
the rain eases and the world smiles its
evil grin.

you'll never make it out alive.

- wonderland

8.

grit your teeth boy

you were made for more than this

hollow existence

- built for better things

9.

stars shine in your eyes and
supernovas dance in your bones.
chaos wrapped in stardust and
gunpowder ; a beautiful disaster

    - on being human with skin too tight

10.

souls are eternal. this we accept as fact.

is it possible that the universe plays with

our lives?

creates a set of events so that two fill

the same space? even for a short time?

does the universe make mistakes?

nothing is infallible, so it must be

possible.

possible for there to be filing errors in

heaven leading to a misalignment of fate

on earth.

two souls so perfectly complementary,

but missing each other by seconds,

days, centuries.

souls are eternal, therefore we might all

just be living for our second chance

at happiness.

- souls meant for more

11.

beware the girls with lions in their hearts

the ones with dragons in their souls

and thunder in their voices

for their minds are utopian jungles

and there is no tolerance for monsters

like you

- monsters that tear everything they

touch into tiny pieces

12.

thunder cracks and lightning flashes

across the sky

you bolt in bed

arm of a lover across your waist

breathing slows as heartbeats race

goosebumps rippling in the breeze

dreams wrest you from slumber and

sent you upright in the dark

visions fading with the storm

you can't remember why

but you are alive

and so are dreams

- dreamers and prophets

13.

the story of you is written on your skin

and few know the language

- even fewer cared to learn

14.

with stars twinkling above you set your

sights on the horizon

the slow turn of the earth steady

beneath your feet

the slow rock of the ship sending you

into Hypnos

love letters folded in your pocket, the

creases well worn

the words faded, yet memorized

but you're coming home
finally coming home

- sailors are hopeless romantics

15.

days pass by and

towns on the interstate

pass in the same fashion;

one after another

in a blink

miles have past.

no memory of them exist

jewels on necklaces are beautiful

chains are dependable

brakes don't work

accelerators work too well.

soon hundreds of towns have gone

and the only thing left

is the highway

- road trip

16.

take me as i am. i have no more masks anymore, you destroyed them all. the storms in my heart are clawing through my voice and raining down my cheeks.

you destroyed me. somehow i left my common sense at the door and i knew it was a mistake, but at the time it didn't look like a mistake.

it felt like hope and adventure and my entire self flew with eagles across the sky. nothing could make me feel that again. i don't expect you to care, not anymore.

so this is me

yelling into the void

take me as i am.

- relearning who i am without you at my

side

17.

pluck the strings of fate and listen to them sing

- do gods make the strings or just play them

18.

there's something to be said for old

books

the ones with spines cracked to

favourite passages

pages edge yellow with time and soft

from countless fingerprints

words nagging in the back of the many

minds

imagine the stories they would tell

all those old books

- history and memories trapped in pages

19.

get angry princess

sharpen your

    tongue

    teeth

    claws

    mind

    blade

do not be afraid to tell the princes

    to go to hell

tell your brother to *fuck off*

yellscreamfight

fight for him

    for you

    for the kingdom

get angry princess

let them fear you

- one day you will be queen

20.

/you believe in aliens?

a laugh a scorn a question

a terrible thought for the human race

a zero sum game

\you don't?/

either we are alone in the universe

with only ourselves for company

a species that is so lonely we build and

create and grow

/no

or we are not the only ones in the stars

that hope and laugh and love

but our messages in the great beyond

do not paint the best picture

so the others think of earth as the

birthplace of savage bloodthirsty beasts

bent on self-destruction

barely out of the soup

\what a sad way to live/

- alone in the universe with only

ourselves to blame

21.

the wide, black road seems endless and

the humid air makes it hard to move

you hear them shuffling and moaning

not far enough behind

their sense of smell keeps them

following the body odour

(as showers were a thing of the past)

one mistake and you're dead

you're dead and you become what

you hunt

such is the way of the world now; the

dead don't know how to stay dead

you joked with your companions that

they looked like death warmed over

it got a laugh,

but those voices are now silenced and

turned to groans in the dark

you almost arrive at your destination -

this time, next time is a gamble

hailed like a hero to fanfare and

celebration, but the gloom and doom

hang in the air

you turn around and fire your weapon-

dead target;

Welcome to America, the land of the

living dead.

- welcome to the new America

ACKNOWLEDGMENTS

This was not a solo process.

Thank you to any piece of television, film, book, game, character, song, or event that inspired me to ask questions and dig deeper.

Thank you to my family and friends who'd help me with grammar and word choice. And endlessly read anything I send them no matter how terrible.

Thank you to all other poets; past, present, and future. Inspiration comes in all forms.

Thank you Michalea Bessey, for the drop dead gorgeous cover art.

Thank you to the team at Alvira Publishing for hosting the #writeyourheartout challenge.

Thank you for picking this up and holding it in your hands.

Immortality is achieved when your name is written down. I have instead written down my mind. Am I immortal now?

ABOUT THE AUTHOR

Dean Wood, the author of Scrap Paper Poetry, received their Master of Science in Forensic Science from Trent University, although the teachings and gory details from forensic science are for a very different collection of words. They are a self-proclaimed "scrap paper poet"; nothing is safe as they will write on anything flat and holds a mark. An Ontario native, Dean is a lover of books, science, nature, and their yellow Labrador, Buddy. This is their first published collection.

Find more of Dean's work on Instagram @fallfromgrace67.